By: Kathleen Davis
Illustrated by: Rekha Salin

Dedicated To:
My two little monsters who never let me sleep
and my "super sidekick" who always has my back

Special Thanks To:
Rekha for all your hard work and
Mia for always being willing to help

There is a superhero
who sometimes can be scared.

He fights the monsters bravely
and seldom needs his lair.

Though creaks and cracks and whirly sounds may sometimes cause a fright,

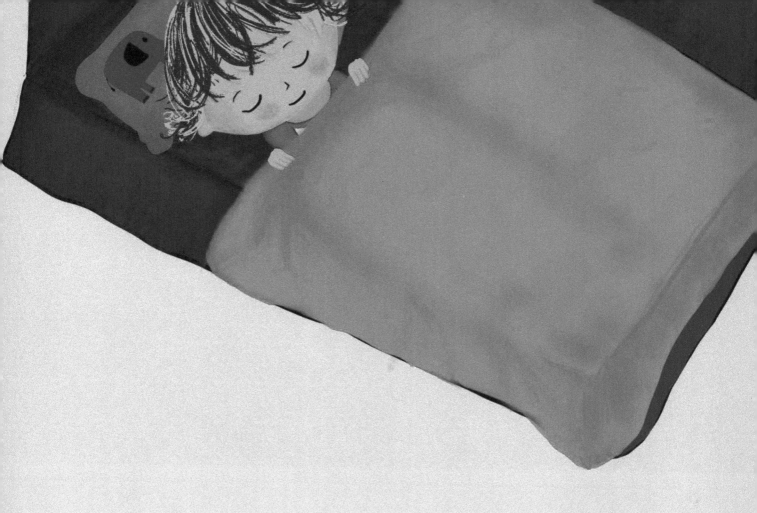

his superhero powers all lead to a good night.

He has a super sidekick
who is sassy as can be.

The monsters fear her wild roar and sometimes so do we.

This sidekick is his best friend
for now and ever more.
They'll always have each other's back,
no matter what's in store.

When wild things come from the night,
they simply tell them "No!"

You can't!
You won't!
You Never
For

No horny beast or fire flames
or slimy claws will hold them back

They'll face them all with sheer delight,
then have a midnight snack.

I know a superhero,
who sometimes can be scared.

He knows there's not
a thing to fear,
for we are always here.

Do not fear, for I am with you.

Isaiah 41:10

I AM BRAVE

I AM STRONG

I AM SAFE

I AM LOVED

I AM BRAVE

CPSIA information can be obtained
at www.ICGtesting.com
Printed in the USA
LVHW071920170622
721563LV00001B/1

By: Kathleen Davis
Illustrated by: Rekha Salin

Dedicated To:
My two little monsters who never let me sleep
and my "super sidekick" who always has my back

Special Thanks To:
Rekha for all your hard work and
Mia for always being willing to help

There is a superhero
who sometimes can be scared.

He fights the monsters bravely
and seldom needs his lair.

Though creaks and cracks and
whirly sounds may sometimes cause a fright,

his superhero powers all lead to a good night.

He has a super sidekick
who is sassy as can be.

The monsters fear her wild roar
and sometimes so do we.

This sidekick is his best friend
for now and ever more.
They'll always have each other's back,
no matter what's in store.

When wild things come from the night,
they simply tell them "No!"

You can't!

You won't!

You Never

You For

No horny beast or fire flames
or slimy claws will hold them back

They'll face them all with sheer delight,
then have a midnight snack.

I know a superhero,
who sometimes can be scared.

He knows there's not
a thing to fear,
for we are always here.

Do not fear, for I am with you.

Isaiah 41:10

CPSIA information can be obtained
at www.ICGtesting.com
Printed in the USA
LVHW071920170622
721563LV00001B/1

9 781736 113202